A Secret Legacy of
Elves and Faeries

POCKET EDITION

Published from
The Joshua Free Imprint – JFI Publications
Mardukite Borsippa HQ, San Luis Valley, Colorado
Founding Church of Mardukite Zuism,
Mardukite Academy & Systemology Society
for religious and educational purposes only.

A Secret Legacy of Elves and Faeries

THE OTHERWORLD INITIATION OF ROBERT KIRK

Based on the work by Joshua Free
and the writings of Robert Kirk
Edited by Rowen Gardner

THE JOSHUA FR...
JFI PUBLIC...

© 2023, JOSHUA FR...

ISBN : 978-1-961509-17-7

ELVENOMICON SERIES-II BOOK-1

Premiere Pocket Paperback — *September 2023*

Mardukite Druidism (Grade-I, D-Series)

mardukite.com

Authentic Elven-Faerie Magick
at your fingertips!

An official companion volume to the original "Elvenomicon" or "Elven-Faerie Grimoire" containing additional high-value esoteric lore drawn from the research of Joshua Free based on the notebooks of Rev. Robert Kirk.

Open the door to the ancient elven tradition and explore the Faerie Realm as guided by the accounts of those who have been there and received direct initiation into its mysteries.

"A Secret Legacy of Elves and Faeries" reveals the significances and occult knowledge hidden within Kirk's "Secret Commonwealth" which was written over 300 years ago.

Joshua Free has been paving the way through the Elven-Faerie glamour of nature magick for over 25 years, and now presents this follow-up to portions of the original "Elvenomicon" as a stand-alone pocket handbook for the first time!

"Secret Legacy of Elves and Faeries" is your key to unlock long-lost magickal wisdom preserved in the most ancient Faerie traditions.

If you desire the best possible guide as your companion for your journey into the original academic presentation of "Commonwealth" (also included herein), then read the "Legacy" today and decide for yourself what is real.

Titles in the newly released
2023 pocket paperback series
based on the "*Elvenomicon*"
by Joshua Free

Published by JFI Publications

TABLET OF CONTENTS

TABLE OF CONTENTS

INTRODUCTION

by Joshua Free

My participation in the legacy behind 'A *Secret Legacy of Elves and Faeries*' began in the mid-1990's amidst critical resurgence of 'New Age' interests—and foremost among these popular revivals: the *Celts* and *Druids*.

A *Secret Legacy of Elves and Faeries* is an integral part of a greater body of work pertaining to my personal involvement with *Elven-Faerie* traditions of Druidism for over 25 years. This material was imparted to me by direct personal 'apprenticeship' with its modern developers as reflected in what I've presented as the first *Elvenomicon* series.

The original '*Elvenomicon*' volume contained a trilogy. It first circulated in the underground as "*The Book of Elven-Faerie*," but I later renamed it *Elvenomicon* to avoid confusing the total collection of work with the title of the first discourse it contained: *Book of Elven-Faerie*—retitled *Secret Book of Elven-Faerie* for this present series reissue. It is a separate discourse from the other two parts in the trilogy: *Greenwood Forest Grimoire* and

The Elven-Faerie Grimoire—the first of which is now released as *"The Enchanted Forest"* for its reissue in a series of individual pocket editions. Collectively, this trilogy comprises *Elvenomicon* 'Series-1' and contains my own original presentation of Elven-Faerie Druidic Tradition, now standing for 20 years past.

The subject of 'Faery-Faiths in Celtic Countries' frequently occupies the attention of Druids throughout the ages, but also practitioners of modern Elven-Faerie magical traditions. The influence on 'New Age' revivals of 'Faery Wicca' and 'Celtic Witchcraft' are equally significant. Many customs and 'sabbats' observed today—and quite often taken for granted—very much owe their foundations to the ancient 'Celtic-Faerie Tradition' and what is better known as *"Druidism."*

"Secret Book of Elven-Faerie" resulted from many years of research, deliberation and contemplation spent in personal dedication to the Elven Tradition before attempting to set this version of it in down in print. It is a companion to '*The Secret Legacy of Elves and Faerie*' in the newer series, derived from deep underground sources—ones that have

never been revealed by any of its initiates, but which is frequently drawn from by the same—as obvious by compositions of many popular New Age titles that emerged during the 1990's. A stand-alone version of this material has never been published before.

The "Elven Way" and "Faerie Tradition" are now a part of nearly all relevant 21st century 'new consciousness', 'new thought' or otherwise earth-oriented forms of 'nature mysticism'. My notes that *this* work is based on—as a *"living testament"*—have been reevaluated numerous times before developing the present publication. It is often difficult to solidify Elven lore and "words of light" to the printed page—for they are fluidly dynamic, shimmering etherically in the waves of the cosmic sea.

Only "Druidry" and indigenous shamanism reflect the same type of spiritual "pathway" for Human Ascension that is alluded to in Elven Tradition. And if supplemented with our latest spiritual developments for "Systemology," an Elven-Faerie Druid Tradition can be an effective stepping stone on this greater Pathway to a Spiritual Ascension.

Although most New Age texts equate Elves and other elemental faerie beings exclusively with the Otherworld or Astral Plane, more experienced practitioners understand the connection between these races and a "very real" legacy of Elven-Dragon traditions and the *Tuatha d'Anu* migrating westward across Europe from Mesopotamia and Anatolia, carrying with them a vast tradition and repository of knowledge from the "Ancient Mystery School." These matters are discussed at length in this volume prepared for Series-I, "*The Book of Elven-Faerie*" or rather, '*The Secret Book of Elven-Faerie*'.

The term "Elven magic" ("Elven magick") is used to distinguish this "Elven-Ffayrie" system—also called the "*Edaphic Tradition*"—from others in the 'New Age'. However, to the Elves themselves, magic *is* simply "magic" and it comes from an innate faculty—not some "supernatural" facet of life or intellectual study. Once again: Magic is *not* a "supernatural" power. On the contrary, magick is quite "natural" and, in this universe, follows principles of "natural law" or "cosmic law" even if not commonly understood.

When Humans refer to "magick," they are simply referring to an esoteric study and a creative use of forces in the Universe—the same principles that manifest reality on a moment-to-moment basis. It is the practical application of the true knowledge and lore in everyday life. It should always be enacted *towards* one's own Ascension and in acts to manifest a harmonious world for all Life.

True "magick" in the Elven Tradition is innate. These beings do not require years of arcane study and training that the Wizard Schools of Humans and "Fey-Touched" must resort to. Elven-Ffayrie simply do not see "magick" as something "outside" of themselves. It is developed and refined as part of their everyday natural life—over a period of progressive self-discovery—just as a Human might choose to refine their own personal tastes and skills, affecting muscle memory or some other artificial *automaticity* for experiencing (and creating) reality.

Wisdom of experience—and I mean Self-Honest experiences from a point of true actualized Awareness—develops with time, and this is something that Elven-Ffayrie races are not short on while residing in the 'Lands Beyond'. Elves and faerie folk also view magick as a part of art. When something created or changed becomes charged or imbued with energy as a result of intention, it becomes art—and the Fey learned to use this art to shape the natural world we see all around us as our "reality." And magick—in all of its forms—will create, transform or even destroy some reflection of our global "reality."

"Magickal feats"—as conceived and purported by Humans—are accomplished via the activation of the mind's subconscious faculties—which becomes "potential power." It may be activated with specific use of symbolism and imagery or focal aids that help an individual direct or channel energy.

We are always actively participating in this *game*—but it is only with our *conscious* participation that we have the power to truly and knowingly by creative.

Many customs and methods of raising energy for this very purpose exist—ritual movements, breathing exercises, ceremonial dances—all of which entice the awareness of the total *Self* to become actively involved in bringing about desired results. All intentional acts are "magical"—even when it is cyclic self-talk of defeatism—and we put our awareness and attention-energies into wherever our focus lies.

All acts, whether mundane or esoteric—are magical when they are movements of energy that create change—in accordance with true will—and following natural laws and cosmic principles that may or may not be widely understood. The Human Condition is easily distracted, and so rituals and ceremonial drama; use of music and vocalized intentions; alternative attire and altar dressings; fragrance of sweet and musty incense and flickering firelight—all are effectively used to bring the *Self* into full awareness and control of the *Self* alone.

It is important to realize—especially if you desire a true understanding of "Elven Magick"—that it is not the rituals and incantations themselves that hold the "power" in magic. A catalyst only represents potential until properly used—and that use is based on ability. "Magickal abilities" come from within—first and foremost—from the part of the "individual" that is not "separated" from the All—but is interconnected and linked absolutely to the fundamental One-ness of reality.

"*The Secret Book of Elven-Faerie*" provides an unparalleled record of the "lost history of Earth"—and the origins for all derived practical applications of Elven-Faerie lore and Druidic magic. As the core volume of the series—and the original "Elvenomicon" anthology—it has already proven its worth and popularity in the underground; stand-ing the test of time for over two decades. This entire series of volumes will certainly continue to inspire aligned realizations and enliven the ongoing traditions of the Elven Way and Faerie Path in perpetuity.

—Joshua Free, Summer Solstice 2023
San Luis Valley, Colorado

THE SECRET
LEGACY

# of mortals and elves: the secret legacy of robert kirk

Previously in these books, we have mainly concerned ourselves with esoteric information and mystic lore regarding phenomenon of Elven-Faerie 'transitions' and encounters with Elemental Beings in the "physical world"—"surface world" or "Lands Above" —perceived by mortal Humans.

The secret legacy of Reverend Robert Kirk is amazing—and unique—because it chronicles Elven lore from the *other side*—from a man who physically entered the Otherworld, became an initiate of the Elven-Ffayrie Tradition and returned to *our side* able to share it—at least, for a time and in some guise or another. We are not referring here to "mental/astral travel" or the type of "guided meditations" that run rampant in "New Age" 'How-To' books for *"entering the fairylands."* Original journal records and accounts of Robert Kirk's experiences are unparalleled in recent history.

Robert Kirk gained admittance to the "Otherworld," accessing the "Elven Libraries" on repeated occasions—not simply by happenstance or coincidence. He was even allowed to keep a sketch-diary journal to account for his experiences—which have now been widely circulated in various editions.

Elemental and/or mortal "transitions"—or any contact with "nature spirits"—requires appropriate conditions or natural circumstances in addition to skills in directing or channeling currents of energy. During appropriate times, Robert Kirk was able to return to the same "Faerie Howe," or Hollow Hill and gain entrance at will. We make mention of these things here to entice you —but the story of Robert Kirk truly should begin, well, at the beginning...

****

Born in the year 1644, Robert Kirk was the *seventh son* of an Episcopalian minister and later even became a minister himself, in his home parish of Aberfoyle—Perthshire, Scotland. Although notably a devout Christian, Kirk spent his life interested and influenced by Elven-Faerie lore—though his religion did not permit him to accept the "magical" and "occult" aspects of the actual tradition. He did, however, see the importance in preserving Celtic lore and ancient Irish-Gaelic language—even overseeing a Gaelic translation of the Judeo-Christian *Holy Bible*, personally translating the *Psalms* and *Proverbs*. Kirk's missionary life reflected the *Bardic Culdee* of the distant past, those that once preserved authentic Celtic and Druidic symbolism in the *Book of Kells*, an "illuminated" manuscript copy of the Four Gospels written in the Gaelic language.

It is evident that Robert Kirk never intended on becoming a monumental "New Age" figure—or advocate for 'occultism' and active "mystery traditions" revived today in favor of the Elven Way. His writings do display some personal familiarity with archaic Hermetic-Gnostic lore and Rosicrucian doctrines—making a direct reference to several in his most popularly known treatise: "*The Secret Commonwealth of Elves, Fauns and Fairies.*" The precise nature of Kirk's personal background remains unclear—but he likely had access to many obscure Celtic manuscripts and other esoteric documents as an esteemed member of the Christian Clergy. It is likely that his strict religious upbringing resulted in a reluctance to delve into metaphysical matters—and it comes as no surprise that his "pagan" interests were of noted concern to his father.

The infamous "Faerie Howe"—where Robert Kirk's body was eventually found—was a location that he visited frequently throughout his life. But, one day, Kirk actually discovered, or rather, had revealed to him, the entrance to the "Faerieland Otherworld." By means of a special knock at the right 'threshold' times of month and day, Kirk would be granted repeated access to an alternate dimension—called by many names throughout lore: the *Elflands*, the *Faerieland*, the *Faerieworld*, the *Otherworld*, just to name a few.

In his published accounts, Kirk does not always refer to these matters—especially concerning the Otherworld—in first person. He prefers instead to attribute the accounts, lore and traditions to those seers and mystics interviewed as part of his research. No

doubt there were many political and esoteric reasons for such anonymity, especially
during this time in history. Kirk based his
literary work on journals dated from 1688-
1692, implying four years of practical "Otherworld Initiation" that complimented his
research in folklore—at a time when, just
across the pond in newly founded puritan
America, people were burned at the stake
for even speaking of such things.

Robert Kirk's *"Secret Commonwealth of Elves"*
was never published in its complete state—
and never revealed to the public at all during Kirk's lifetime. Some scholars believe
that all of the first person references concerning mysticism, the Otherworld Tradition and Elven-Ffayrie encounters, were re-
placed in the published version as second-
hand accounts from "seers"—or edited out
of the "official" manuscript altogether—before its eventually distribution to a 17th
century predominantly Christian society as
authored by a Christian minister.

In spite of this, Kirk emphasizes and insists
that there is no real conflict between his
own religious beliefs and what he learns

concerning the Elven-Ffayrie tradition. The only real contradiction emerges from the minds of Fundamentalist Christians that see these beings only as the demons and devils of their own paradigm or worldview. Kirk even goes as far as to say that he feels that it is his God-given mission in life to clarify misconceptions concerning the fey among his human Christian brethren.

It may be that the Antiquarian writers of Robert Kirk's time—the Brothers' Grimm, John Aubrey, John Toland and Iolo Morgan-wg, just to mention a few—all felt that there was a very real part of folklore and Elven-Faerie Tradition hidden within the secret folds of Nature—and that it was quickly disappearing from the consciousness of contemporary society, and therefore required advocates supporting its preservation.

****

After one disturbing encounter in Faerie-land—concerning a chance episode with a solitary *Dark Elf*—Robert Kirk took it upon himself to seek out the city of the *Unseelie Court* and attempt to apologize for the rise in tension resulting from his appearance in the Otherworld. Apparently, he had not yet realized that by even setting foot on the grounds of the *Dark Elves*, he was in violation of the most severe *Unseelie* laws. The *Unseelie Court* immediately sentenced him to death—but the *Seelie Court* intervened, altering their judgment, ultimately deciding that Kirk should remain forever a "prisoner" in the Otherworld, and this permanent "transition" would still leave his physical body dead in the "Middle World." He is then allowed only one night to return to the "Lands Above" to set his affairs in order —being allowed to leave in good faith—then during this time he leaves his journals behind for his son and returns to the "Lands Below" to serve out his sentence.

Some time after Kirk's death, he makes a spiritual appearance to a relative—claiming he will again appear at the Christening of her daughter. He states that at that time, her husband is to throw an iron dagger at his apparition—if he does so, then the enchantment of the Faerieland would be broken and he could return to the "Middle World."

According to the accounts that followed—when the Christening came and Kirk's spirit did appear, those who were present were so astounded that they did not move to throw a dagger and so Kirk remained in the Other-world.

Years later, Kirk makes his second spiritual attempt to communicate—this time with a different family occupying the house Kirk once resided in. His apparition informs them that they are to baptize their child in his writing room and stab a dagger in the seat of the chair Kirk sat in to write—which apparently remained in the room. According to the apparition, if they were to do this, he would be free. But, again, this is not even attempted and Kirk is never freed. Although easy to dismiss, these accounts do reflect behaviors that we might actually expect from the population at that time—or it may be that an eternity in the Otherworld was Kirk's destiny.

the quest for the otherworld

Mortals seeking encounters with nature-bound spirits—such as the Elven-Ffayrie—should first start by immersing themselves in natural valleys, untouched woodlands and virgin forests. By this, we mean those places where Humans are not falling trees and houses are not being developed—or even in view. Also avoid places overrun by "electromagnetic" transmissions through power lines and satellite dishes which can cause mystic-interference.

While smaller and urban parks are nice for walks, picnics, or maybe even studying, meditation or working with a specific tree current—most of these have been planned, planted and are arranged and maintained with little left to grow wild. They are also usually host to too much Human foot traffic and activity to make for the best places to meditate or connect with Nature—and especially those spirits that inhabit it. Other titles in this series also provide numerous examples of inviting "Faerie" into your life.

Make certain your own foot traffic is light and quiet—walking slow and deliberately—being sure not to disturb the natural vibrations of the environment.

To achieve the desired results, your energy must be in alignment (meaning, resonant or synchronous) with Nature—so a practitioner of the Elven-Faerie tradition does well to take care that they are not disrupting the 'natural flow' of Nature, or disturbing wildlife with unnecessary fast movement, ruckus or chatter. If the visible "Green World" you *can* see is disrupted by your presence, then you can rest assure that the same sentiment is shared by the "Nature-spirits." They carry a disdain for Human noise—so stop, sit and *shut up* often— perhaps with your back against a tree. Be patient. You may wish to practice certain breathing exercises or any meditations that will calm your vibrations and put you in tune with frequencies matching your surroundings. Calm your body; still your mind—activate a 'light body' and 'light shield' if you are proficient in such esoterica from other titles of this series—but the key here, no matter the technique involved—is to *increase awareness*.

During the course of your personal journey —ventures, experiments and experiences— should you happen upon a natural physical entrance to the Otherworld, lore suggests that you should not disturb it, or do anything immediately at first. Stop and wait. Watch and be patient, again. If nothing changes, try encircling it nine times and then waiting some more at the "doorway." You might then try knocking three times— making certain it will not disturb anything loose. Another secret knock sequence that is applicable here is: 1-2-3 or /-//-///.

If an initiate is not given a "portal key" by direct personal apprenticeship with Elven-Ffayrie folk, the only other available option is trial and error. Do not, however, be a menace—this will only work against your efforts. After three passive attempts, an alternative is to set up a "Circle of Power" to help meditate and calm your mind—and if you desire, practice Elemental magick rites —"opening portal thresholds" or "calling the quarters"—whatever your preferred means of summoning Elemental powers or currents of energy with ritual applications. Fey folk are commonly attracted to Elemental Magick because it specifically validates and acknowledges their existence, asks for their assistance and utilizes energy streams they are akin to.

While selecting areas of exploration in the forest, keep in mind that certain Elven-Ffayrie types are especially attracted to places where land meets water. These might be ponds, streams, waterfalls, or the archetypal "babbling brook." Lore suggests that these places carry intensive connectivity that links the physical world with the astral plane or Otherworld—making them very common places of spiritual encounter.

The element of water is among the most sacred in Elven tradition—for its "life-giving" qualities—as is the 'air' we breathe. Running water is specifically related to irrigation—which is an essential aspect of agricultural work and gardening—a skill mastered famously in the Ancient Near East and carried across Europe as the populations transformed from nomadic hunter-gathers into settled farmers. "Nature-spirits" and agriculture carry a long-standing tradition together. Naturally, living closer to the natural Elemental world allowed early "pagan" cultures to experience more significant encounters with the Elemental beings and "Nature-spirits" sharing an affinity with the planet Earth.

Elemental Spirits and Nature-beings encountered in magical practices are typically neutral in polarity and crystalline in nature. This means that they are generally charged with an energy type that mirrors the polarity of willpower, intention and emotional energy discharged by a Mystic, Druid, or Wizard, &tc. This is essentially how power of thoughtforms operates and how the psyche divides oneness into polarities of "good" and "evil." Hence, rituals "of the light" will attract spirits of a like nature —and those dark sacrificial ceremonies of cult abuse, that we often hear about in horror stories, will generate intense emotional resonance with "evil" polarities. Energy—as the Wizard understands it—is basically a catalyst of "attraction" operating on the "principle of like-forces." A ritual, rite or meditation will attract the same type of energy that is radiated from its conductance— if successful.

Nature-Wizards and Shamans often use sages and sweetgrass as an incense smoke to clear an area of unwanted, static or negatively charged energies.

Another "Faerie" formula is ash, elder and hawthorne—burned in equal parts. This also aids in charging an area with a vibrational resonance that is more likely to attract the Sylvanus Folk—if that is your desire.

The fey folk are attracted to small shiny objects, mirrors and trinkets. They are also partial to the colors: green, red, blue and yellow. Natural folk-style acoustic music is sure to entice them.

Remember that the Elven-Ffayrie are traditionally interested in celebrations of life and love—so you must invite them to bright shinning places that are not somber or negative in any way. Only once you have made your own *life* a place that is fit to include such experiences, will it be possible to make it your *reality*.

MARDUKITE MASTER COURSE ACADEMY LECTURE #20[*]

"otherworld tech"

The "Route of Druidism and the Dragon Legacy" is actually of such richness and color that you really could formulate a "Druid School" exclusively from that—or at least, quite an extensive curriculum for your "Wizard School."

In fact, it's been designed in such a way, that for example, *Merlyn's Complete Book of Druidism* and the Master materials that compose this, is actually a qualifying "Grade-I" access-point for those that seek it—for those that prefer this to the broader study of the "magical curriculum" and "ritual magick" and "ceremonial traditions" of all that in the Western Magical Tradition (that are explored in Route-A).

---

[*] Transcript of a lecture given by Joshua Free on September 23, 2020; revised from "*Druids, Elves & Dragons: Mardukite Master Course Academy Lectures (Volume II)*"—also contained in "*The Complete Mardukite Master Course.*"

Honestly, this has been designed, and this Master Edition textbook here has been designed, so that if necessary, *this* can be someone's introduction to "Magick & Mysticism" in addition to the "Route of Druidism & Dragon Legacy" that all leads into Grade-II.

Now, *you* being a "Master Instructor" and this being the "Master Course" and to be "*Certified*" in being able to instruct all Grades is to *know* all Grades, but when it comes to individual Seekers and it comes to bringing those onto the *Pathway to Self-Honesty* or as those enter into Mardukite Zuism or even the Academy of Systemology or the Systemology Society, we don't actually require that an individual work through Route-A. It does make exceptional reference material and background and a core foundation for doing the rest—there is no substitute, single source substitute, for *The Great Magickal Arcanum* out there today.

But for those who end up—their introduction or their entry-point onto the *Pathway*—ends up being the "Nature Magic," "Druidism," the "Dragon Tradition," "Celtic Faerie," any of this... just go ahead and use this as the

Grade-I work and emphasize that which they're showing the inclinations in.

"*The Elven-Faerie Grimoire*" of the '*Elvenomicon*' series is, by itself, essentially a complete "ritual guide" for an individual to follow their traditional use of "practical magick," "ritual magic"—the same kind of flavor of work that we were discussing previously in lectures a couple of days ago. It's essentially an entire "Book of Shadows, Light and Enchantment" or *grimoire* for practicing within "Elven-Faerie" or "Faerie-Druid" tradition.

"Druid Magic" and "Elven Magic" places a lot of emphasis on incorporating Nature in any 'magical work', or communing with Nature, spending time in Nature, observing Nature, in order to essentially be "grounded" as an individual. 'Grounding' being one of the core fundamentals of operating any other work. And any other work can be done from, you know, as an Actualized Alpha-Spirit.

All you need to be doing is making sure you're grounded and in complete communication, control and command of the body; and then be able to operate from the point-of-view of the Alpha-Spirit. And this could easily be done when working in Nature, free of a lot of the worldly distractions, free of any disturbances—being able to achieve the first core of any higher-level work, which is essentially *grounding* and *centeredness* and being able to move out from there. We see that emphasis within any of the ritual texts or the "magick" that's presented in the '*Elvenomicon*' series.

Now, in terms of any "Magic Tech," "Ritual Tech"—anything along those lines; practical applications—well, "Druidism" is a little bit more "intuitive" in its applications of the "mystical traditions." In fact, it's a little bit more of a "mystical" tradition than a "magical" tradition.

With proper application, we start to see a bridge to higher applications routed in the authority of the individual as Self and their empowerment, their understanding, realizations, and their ability to actually *be* in a state of *knowing* true knowledge, that enables and empowers their skills and abilities and what they do went they go about treating the natural world, okay? Which is a little bit different from the more traditional rigorous ritual ceremonial formulas and particular times of day and astrological signs, in which we see other traditions a little bit more fixed in what they are intending to do in their ritual texts or their "magick."

In this case, you're dealing with, really, not as much of a rigorous roll-call of "rules" and "requirements" and "steps" as you are establishing that personal relationship—personal communion—with Nature, with the natural Elements, with, basically the "Cosmos" in essence, as you move your way up. In that relationship—in that *knowingness*—being able to have a better mastery and control of the experience of the material world.

In terms of the "New Age" concept of accessing, you know, the "Faerieland" or so forth, what you'd find in most "New Age" 'How-To' books—most of which involve some sort of mental or astral travel; but, it's really descriptive scripts—what they will refer to as "guided meditations."

I mean, you'll find books just *filled*, hundreds of pages, of guided meditations—almost just reads like a "novel" of stuff. I mean, I don't know what... if they intended to record them

and have them played back or you're sup-
posed to remember all this stuff or just read
through them, because honestly, probably
the biggest benefit you'd have in reading
through them—or any use whatsoever—is
that they might be actually "restimulative"
to some kind of memory recall triggering, or
past-life thing, or some experience that's
been forgotten or filtered out.

But, you could just as soon get that same
stuff reading anything else or just watching
many of the shows or movies that are available out there—would almost yield the same
effect; and that's basically just increasing the
acceptance or Awareness or concept or possibility or parameter within the realm of
mental imagery, or within the realm of reality—within the realm, grasp, hold and reach
of what's considered possible, that someone
may be able to have these, kinda, "Gates" or
"access points" open up to them.

Because prior to that, until someone knows
it's, again, possible or real or any actual aspect to it, then there is nothing to behold.
Suddenly an individual begins to read novels
or watch TV or play various fantasy-oriented

games, all of which have certain themes, it very well may end up "restimulating" certain imprints, certain programming, various implants—even 'past-life' recall—concerning not only times here on this planet when such things were present or there was more mysticism or certain themes or icons were present, but also in other civilizations and times on this planet and even distant pasts and even *before* incarnations on *this* Earth and so on and so forth.

It's for those reasons that some people get... you've heard of some of the "dangers" or you've seen the propaganda about some of the "inherent dangers" to some of this; and that's really all it is. Those who aren't really able to *handle* some of the mental imagery or the triggers of the "restimulation" of who they are—sometimes really have, without guidance, and again this is where a Master would really come in handy, they begin to lose themselves in it; or they lose touch with what's really going on, because they "restimulate" something, which is very real to them, and it was probably very real when it happened, but it's not present right now, is it?

And so a lot of times individuals get kind of "keyed in" or "trapped" or "locked into" specific modes because they've been "turned on" and they're being handled as if it's happening *now*, because for whatever reason it wasn't handled at the time or it hasn't been managed or it's been suppressed to the point where it's—the pressures are just, it can't be ignored anymore.

But one way or another, "keyed-in" stuff has to be faced and handled. As we step back to view these various traditions and histories and then even going into Mesopotamia (in Grade-II) and where some of the implanting for *this* current civilization first occurred—you are definitely running into many elements that could be "restimulative," that could trigger various responses, reactions or complete 'phase-shifts' to where someone or some aspect is flipped on like a switch.

Now *you*, from a Grade-III perspective—as a Systemologist—is actually able to treat these circumstances and this phenomenon, you know, far better and more effective and valuable to a Seeker, than we have ever been able to do before when we were only working with these systems and traditions within what we consider the Grades they are in.

Being true to this idea that we're treating a Master-level understanding of anything that could be considered "practical tech" or "authentic tech" in this level (or in this area), really it would be impossible to sidestep at least one case study that *is* explored within *Book of Elven-Faerie* material—and *The Secret Legacy of Elves and Faeries*—of course, referring to the legacy and life of Robert Kirk.

****

Robert Kirk—or Reverend Robert Kirk—is a 17th Century "case study" that we use to explore the encounters between "mortals" and "Elves." Robert Kirk—he was born in 1644—he was the seventh son of an Episcopalian minister; he was born in Scotland. He also became a minister.

His work titled "*Secret Commonwealth of Elves, Fauns & Faeries*" is actually one of the few real reference points that an individual has when exploring any kind of historical background for revival of, for example, the 'Elven Tradition' or 'Faerie Tradition'—because in that material we learn about such things as the Seelie Court and Unseelie Court, the Faerie Courts, Faerie Traditions, beliefs, practices, customs—all things regarding the "Faerie."

Much of this is actually synthesized in the material for the '*Elvenomicon*' series. It's *not* a baseless tradition that I sought to establish—much like we're doing in Mardukite Zuism in bringing 'Mesopotamian Tradition' and aspects and explorations of our most ancient literature on the planet into the "Neopagan" realm. What I did with the *Book of Elven-Faerie* and *Elvenomicon* material was essentially integrate a complete tradition of Elven and Faerie Druidism.

Concerning source-material we have from Robert Kirk—now, you got to remember: his public work is being presented as... Well, don't forget: he's a member of the clergy—and he's writing particularly for a nation or society that is predominantly Christianized. And so most of the explorations and any of his personal encounters or opinions are actually passed off as being those of, for a example, a "seer" or given "according to an account of interview" with someone else.

Best we can tell, from 1688 until 1692, Kirk experienced some kind of actual four-year long encounter—or initiation—into the Otherworld, this 'Faerieland'; and was able to actually record much of what he discovered. And the thing is: unlike what you might find today, in terms of 'fame' and 'fortune', this was not something he divulged openly, or even capitalized on. "*Secret Commonwealth*" was not even published during his lifetime. He certainly wasn't trying to delude anyone or make any personal claims.

Most of Robert Kirk's encounters are connected to what we know today as a "Faerie Mound" or "burial mound"—an ancient ancestral "burial mound"—in Scotland. Some of the locals referred to them as "Faerie Hills" and they had a long tradition—a long legacy —for example, the locals would tell children, "Don't get caught going to close to the Fairy Hills," you know, things of that nature. And these places already had... Well, people knew there was something about them; that there was something different about them or that they had some significance. Of course, the nature and semantics of these beliefs have shifted across time and various cultures.

The end result of Robert Kirk's recorded life is interesting, but in many ways, also disturbing. He ends up trespassing in Unseelie territory while in the Otherworld. As a result of his encounter with a Dark Elf, he's actually sentenced to 'death', so to speak—and instead is actually claimed by... he's vouched for by the Seelie Court; and so they eventually decide that he can remain alive as a prisoner, and thereafter forever inhabit what he referred to as the "Lands Below."

In *his* accounts, the Faerieland is referred to as the 'Lands Below', and the surface world—that which is the physical world of humanity and where things take place on the surface of the Earth—is called the 'Lands Above'. And that's the distinction. The term 'Otherworld' isn't actually used; that's just a word that I often apply. And, of course, "Faerieland" is simply, again, another one of the terms that we might use when we are describing this.

Kirk is sentenced to serve out his remaining existence in the 'Lands Below'. He's given time to set his affairs in order; he's given one night to return to the 'Lands Above' on good faith, of course, that he's going to come back to serve his sentence. And thus, he prepared his manuscripts and journals and sketchbooks for posterity—for his son. In fact, the original *"Secret Commonwealth"* publication ends with a 'note' directing a reader to "see the rest in a little manuscript belonging to Colin Kirk"—presumably the name of Kirk's son, as Andrew Lang states in the 1893 printing of *"Secret Commonwealth"* that he edited.

What we can be certain of, is that the following morning, Kirk's body was found next to the "Faerie Hill." We cannot be absolutely certain of the nature of the 'transitioning'—it's very possible that his encounters with the Otherworld (or the Lands Below or this particular Faerie Realm) were not altogether "terrestrial"; that is was not necessarily that a physical "doorway" opened up and he literally walked down beneath the "soil."

Because one of the things he does write, is that the "Lands Below" were actually very similar—if not more "vivid"—to the Lands Above; that it had its own sky; that it had its own skyscapes that changed with night and day and so forth. And so from that we would have to assume that it is perhaps a different dimension; and for all intents and purposes *probably* the "Magical Universe"—something that we only really just touch upon in the Master Course, but of which we're exploring much more deeply at higher Systemological levels and Grades of the Academy.

And so in terms of *"beings"* or *"entities"*: we know that this "Other" existence... we know that it is possible to transition between existences and that *beings* have an ability to inhabit or take on physical bodies or genetic vehicles as needed. But, we don't know for certain that all individuals are equally Actualized for this ability. Because an *"entity"* or *"spirit"* is not permitted much true freedom without being to a point where an individual could pick up and set down the command of bodies and continue a spiritual existence and later pick up a body again and so on.

We don't know that these were literally physical transitions into an Otherworld as a "body" or that each time that Reverend Kirk was encountering—and later inhabiting this Faerieland during these encounters—that his "body" wasn't being left back here and that this wasn't just simply a very surrealistic use of "transference of the point-of-view." To accomplish this requires an ability to actually "exteriorize" from the "interior" perspective or Awareness of the Human Condition.

Most individuals entrapped in the Human Condition are only able to maintain a point-of-view or Awareness from a physical body. We consider alternate—"higher"—potential for a point-of-view in higher Grades of Systemology; but applying such an understanding certainly elevates the realizations accessible on these matters.

The ability to actually 'transition' consciousness—knowingly—to another level of '*Beingness*' is far more understandable when we consider the 'condensation' or 'descent' of "Universes." Any type of kabbalistic model or sequentially-layered cosmology—even the understanding of 'chakras'—all suggests that a "higher" order of operations ensues back of and behind the visible phenomenon perceived of the 'Lands Above' or *this* world.

Taking our esoteric knowledge base collectively into consideration, we can at least theorize that there is a bridge between the original and basic existential state of what we call the Alpha-Spirit in our Systemology—or the "I-AM" or "Self"—and "*physical existence.*" There are levels and gradients of perception or 'Spiritual Awareness' between the actual *Self* or "Alpha-Spirit" and the experiences of reality through these successive Universes. And our Systemology describes this certain 'trail' or 'track' or 'timeline' that has taken *effect* on the individual—on their *Knowingness* and *Beingness*, or at least the perceptions or considerations on the "reality" thereof.

This 'timeline' or 'track' is compulsively created and carried by us as Alpha-Spirits; and it provides an illusion of sequential time by storing particular incidents as imprinted information. The 'weight' and 'mass' of this 'line' accumulates each step of the way—tying us to lower and lower 'considerations'.

So, it's very possible then, that each and every one of us that's occupying a consideration of a point-of-view of the Human Condition in *this* existence, has formerly occupied considerations of *Beingness* in this 'other' existence. All of this, again, boiling down to the basic 'considerations' for what is "*reality.*"

And for most individuals, the memory of this has been blotted out—and, of course, any actualized ability or responsibility and 'conscious control' over it; the ability to move between "Universes"; or to again occupy this other higher universe that we once occupied before descending to the reality agreements that has fixed our attentions to this lower one—forgetting that we 'made' that choice; that these are conscious decisions or consequences of considerations along the way.

And one of the keys—one of the higher level keys behind any of this work, when we consider what's possible or what's taken place— is that we are trying to move back to *that* point from *this* point. And to do so, we are very much mirroring what we consider the *Pathway to Self-Honesty* or the *Ladder of Ascension* in our Systemology. And so in that, we can see a mirror of us getting back to these roots—getting back to the heart of where we came from. In tracing back along this legacy and map that has been left behind, we might find our route back out; and even more than this—that we might have the certainty and courage to follow that *Pathway* and return to our truest spiritual source-point.

THE SECRET
COMMONWEALTH

THE SECRET COMMONWEALTH
—or—
A Treatise displaying the Chief Curiosities
as they are in Use among the Diverse
People of Scotland to this day;
Singularities for the most Part peculiar
to that Nation.
BY MR. ROBERT KIRK, Minister at Aberfoyle

Here is provided an essay of the
nature and actions of the subterranean (and, for the most part) invisible people, heretofore going under
the name of ELVES, FAUNES, and
FAIRIES, or the like, among the low-
country Scots, as they are described
by those who have the SECOND
SIGHT; and now, to occasion further
inquiry, collected and compared, by
a circumspect inquirer residing
among the Scottish-Irish in Scotland.

of the subterranean inhabitants

These *siths* or fairies—they call *sleagh maith* or 'the good people', it would seem, to ward off their ill attempts (for the Irish 'bless' all they fear harm of) and are said to be of a middle nature between 'man' and 'angel', as we daemons thought to be of old, of intelligent studious spirits, and light, changeable bodies (like those called 'astral') similar to the nature of a condensed cloud and best seen in the twilight.

These bodies are so pliable via the subtlety of the 'spirits' that agitate them, that they can make them appear or disappear at will. Some have bodies or 'vehicles' so spongy, thin and pure, that they are fed only by some fine spiritous liquors that pierce like pure air or oil. Others feed more substantially on '*foison*' [what can be harvested from something] or by the essence of 'corn' or on the 'corn' itself that grows on the surface of the earth, which these fairies steal away—in part, invisibly, and partly preying on the 'grain' as do cows and mice.

In this same age, they are sometimes heard to bake bread, strike hammers—performing such services within the little hillocks they reside. In previous times, before the Gospel dispelled paganism, and in some barbarous places as yet, they enter houses after all are at rest and set the kitchens in order, cleaning all the vessels. Such drudges go under the name of *"Brownies."* When we have plenty, they have scarcity at their homes, and on the contrary; their robberies notwithstanding, they often collect up great stacks of 'corn' for its owners.

Their bodies of congealed air are sometimes carried aloft, otherwise walking in different shapes, and may enter any cranny or cleft of the earth (where air enters)—to their ordinary dwellings, the earth being full of cavities and cells; all places being inhabited by some creature or animal, living in or upon, as there is no such thing as a "pure wilderness" in the whole universe.

We then (the more terrestrial kind), have now so numerously planted all countries, also do labors for those 'hidden people' as well as for ourselves. Albeit when several countries were uninhabited by us, these had their easy tillage in wide open fields, wood and forests.

They remove to other lodgings at the beginning of each quarter of the year, so transversing until doomsday—being impatient to stay in one place and finding some relief by sojourning and changing habitations. Their chameleon-like bodies swim in the air near the earth with bag and baggage. And at such revolution of time, "seers" (or those with 'second sight') have very terrifying encounters with them, even on the highways.

The Scottish-Irish usually shun to travel abroad at these four seasons of the year and thereby have made it a custom to this day to keep church duly every first Sunday of the quarter, to 'hallow' themselves—and their 'corns' and 'cattle'—from the shot and stealth of these wandering tribes. And many of these superstitious people will not be seen in church again till the next quarter begin, as if no duty were to be learned or done by them, but still they pursue the use of worship and sermons to save them from these arrows that fly in the dark.

The Fae are distributed in tribes and orders and have children, nurses, marriages, trials, deaths and burials, equal in appearance to our own (unless they do so for a mock-show or to prognosticate such things among us).

They are clearly seen by those with the Second Sight to eat at funerals and banquets. Hence many of the Scottish-Irish will not taste meat at these meetings, or they will have communion with, or be poisoned by, them. So are they seen to carry the bier or coffin with the corpse among the middle earth men [humans] to the grave.

Some of those with the Sight (whether by art or nature) have told me they have seen at these meetings a 'double-man' or the shape of some man in two places; that is to say, a superterranean and a subterranean inhabitant perfectly resembling one another in all points. They vouch that every element and different state of being have animals resembling those of another element, as there are fish sometimes at sea resembling monks of late order in all their hoods and dresses; just as the Roman invention of good and bad daemons and guardian angels particularly assigned, is called by them an ignorant mistake sprung from this original.

They call this reflex-man a 'Co-Walker', in every way like the man, as a twin-brother and companion, haunting him as his shadow, as is often seen and known among men (resembling the original) both before and after the original is dead, and was also often seen to enter a house, by which these people knew that the person of that likeness was to visit them within a few days.

This copy, echo, or living picture goes at last to his own herd. It accompanied that person so long and frequently for ends best known to itself, whether to guard him from the secret assaults of some of its own folks or only to counterfeit all his actions.

However, the stories of old witches prove that there are all sorts of people with spirits which assume light airy bodies, or "crazed" bodies co-acted upon by foreign spirits, all seem to have some pleasure (at least to relieve pain or melancholy) by striking and capering like satyrs, whistling and screeching (like unlucky birds) in their unhallowed 'synagogues' and '*sabboths*'.

If invited and earnestly required, these companions make themselves known and familiar to humans. Otherwise, being in a different state and element, they neither can nor will easily converse with them. It is said that a *heluo*—a great eater or glutton—has a voracious *Elf* to be his attender, called a *'Joint-Eater'* or *'Just-Halver'*, feeding on the pith or quintessence of what the man eats, and therefore he continues to be lean.

Yet it would seem that they convey the food substance elsewhere, for the subterraneans eat little in their dwellings; their food being exactly clean and served up by pleasant children like enchanted puppets. What food they extract from us is conveyed to their homes by secret paths.

Their houses are called large and fair and (unless at some odd occasions) unperceivable by vulgar eyes—like *Rachland** and other enchanted islands—having for lights continual lamps and fires, often seen without fuel to sustain them.

---

*   *Rathlin Island*—a small "L"-shaped island off the coast of Northern Ireland. [Presumed by editor.]

Women are still alive who tell they were taken away when in 'child-bed' to nurse *Fairie* children, a lingering voracious image of theirs being left in their place (like their reflection in a mirror), which (as if it were some insatiable spirit in an assumed body) made first semblance to devour the meat that it cunningly carried by and then left the carcass as if it expired and departed thence by a natural and common death. The child and fire, with food and other necessities, are set before the nurse as soon as she enters, but she neither perceives any passage out, nor sees what those people do in other rooms of the lodging. When the child is weaned, the nurse dies, or is conveyed back, or gets the choice to stay there.

But if any superterraneans [surface-dwellers] be so subtle as to practice 'sleights' for procuring a privacy to any of the Fae mysteries (such as making use of their ointments, rings which make them invisible or nimble, or casts them into a trance, or alters their shape, or makes things appear at a vast distance, &tc.), they smite them without pain, as with a puff of wind, and relieve them of their natural and acquired 'sights' in the twinkling of an eye, or they strick them dumb.

The Northerners ['*tramontanes*'] to this day, put bread, the Bible, or a piece of iron, in a woman's bed while traveling to save them from being 'stolen'; and they commonly report that all uncouth unknown 'wights' are terrified by nothing earthly as much as cold iron. They suppose the reason to be that Hell lies betwixt the chill tempests and the firebrands of scalding metals and iron of the north (hence the loadstone causes a tendency to that point).

By an antipathy thereto, these odious far-seeing creatures shrug and fright at all that is perceived which relates to so abhorred a place—where their torment is either begun or feared to come hereafter.

Their apparel and speech is like that of the people and country under which they live; so are they seen to wear plaids and variegated garments in the Highlands of Scotland—and *suanochs* (garments made of tartan) in Ireland. They speak little, and that by way of whistling, clear, not rough. The very 'devils' conjured in any country do answer in the language of the place, yet sometimes the subterraneans speak more distinctly than at other times.

Their women are said to 'spin' very finely—to dye, to tissue, and embroider: but whether it is a manual operation of substantially refined 'stuffs' with apt and solid instruments, or only curious cobwebs, impalpable rainbows, and a fantastic imitation of the actions of more terrestrial mortals; since it transcended all the senses of the "seer" to discern whether, I leave it to conjecture as I found it.

Their men travel much abroad, either presaging or aping the dismal and tragical actions of some amongst us, and have also many disastrous doings of their own, as convocations, fighting, gashes, wounds, and burials, both in the earth and air. They live much longer than we, yet die at last, or at least vanish from that state.

It is one of their tenets that nothing perishes, but (as the sun and year) everything goes in a circle, lesser or greater, and is renewed and refreshed in its revolutions. It is another tenet that every "body" in creation moves (which is a sort of 'life'); and further that nothing moves but has another animal moving on it, and so on and on, to the utmost minutest corpuscle that is capable to be a receptacle of life.

They are said to have aristocratic rulers and laws, but no discernible religion, love or devotion towards 'God'. They disappear whenever they hear 'His' name invoked, or the name of 'Jesus' (at which all do bow willingly or by constraint that dwell above or beneath within the earth, *Philippians 2.10*) nor can they act ought at that time after hearing of that sacred name.

The *tabhaisver*, or seer, corresponding with these kinds of familiars, can bring them to appear with a spell, as readily as the Endor Witch to those of her kind. He says they are ever ready to go on hurtful errands, but seldom will be the messengers of great good to humans. He is not terrified by their sight when he calls them, but seeing them in a surprise (as does often happen) extremely frightens him. They do not do all the harm that they appear to have the power to do, nor are they perceived to be in great pain.

They are said to have many pleasant toyish books, but the operation of these pieces only appears in some *'paroxysms of antic corybantic jollity'* as if ravished and prompted by a new spirit entering into them at that instant, lighter and merrier than their own. Other books they have of *'esoterica'*, as like the Rosicrucian style. They have nothing of the Bible except collected parcels for charms and counter-charms, not to defend themselves, but to operate on other animals, for they are a people invulnerable to our weapons.

Albeit werewolves' and witches' true bodies are (by union of the spirit of nature that runs through all, echoing and doubling the blow towards another) wounded at home when the astral assumed bodies are struck elsewhere—as the strings of a second harp tune to a unison sound though only one be struck; yet these Fae have not a second or so gross a body at all to be so pierced; but as air, which when divided unites again. Or, if they feel pain by a blow, they are better physicians than we are and quickly cure it. They are not subject to sore sickness, but dwindle and decay at about the same age.

They are usually silent and sullen. Some say their continual sadness is because of their pendulous state (like those men in *Luke 13.16*), as uncertain what, at the last revolution, will become of them when they are locked up in an unchangeable condition.

But other men of the 'Second Sight', being illiterate and unwary in their observations, learned from witnessing frolic fits of mirth, that are as acted upon a stage. Some believe the subterranean people to be departed souls attending awhile in this inferior state and clothed with bodies procured through their alms deeds in this life; fluid, active, ethereal "vehicles" to hold them, that they may not scatter, nor wander and be lost in the wholeness or their first nothingness; but if any were so impious as to have given no alms, they say when the souls of such do depart, they sleep in an unactive state until they resume the terrestrial bodies again.

Others, that what the low-country Scot calls a *wraith*—and the Irish, *taibshe*—or "death's messenger" sometimes appearing as a little rough dog, and if crossed or conjured in time, will be pacified by the death of any other creature instead of a sick man), is only exuvious fumes of the man approaching death, exhaled and congealed into various likenesses—as 'ships' and 'armies' are sometimes shaped in the air—and called 'astral bodies', agitated as wildfire with wind; and are neither 'souls', nor counterfeiting spirits. Surely these are a numerous people by themselves, having their own politics.

Their weapons are mostly solid earthly bodies—nothing of iron, but much of stone; similar to yellowish soft flint shaped like a barbed arrowhead, but flung like a "dart" with great force. These armaments (cut by art and tools beyond human) have somewhat of the nature of a thunderbolt, subtly and mortally wounding vital parts without breaking the skin—wounds I have observed in beasts and felt them with my hands. They are not as infallible *Benjamites*, hitting at a hairsbreadth, nor are they wholly unvanquishable, at least in appearance.

Those of that 'Second Sight' do not discover strange things when asked, but at fits and raptures, as if inspired with some genius at that instant, which prior did lurk within or about them. Thus, I have frequently spoke to one of them, who in his transport told he cut the body of one these people in who with his iron weapon and so escaped this onset, yet he saw nothing left behind of that appearing divided body; at other times he outwrestled some of them.

His neighbors often perceived this man to disappear at a certain place, and about one hour after to become visible and discover himself near a bowshot from the first place. It was in that place where he became invisible, said he, that the subterraneans did encounter and combat with him.

They who are unseen, unsanctified or called "fey-doomed" are said to be pierced or wounded with those people's weapons, which makes them do [act] somewhat unlike their former practice, causing a sudden alteration, yet the cause of such remains unperceivable. Nor have they power (either they cannot make use of their natural powers or ask not the heavenly aid) to escape the impending blow.

A man of the 'Second Sight' perceived a person standing by him (found to others' view) wholly gored in blood, and he bid him instantly flee. The man wholly laughed at his art and warning since there was no appearance of danger. He had barely contracted his lips from laughter when his enemy unexpectedly leaped to his side and stabbed him with their weapons.

They also pierce cows or other animals—usually said to be *'Elf-Shot'*—whose purest substance (if they die) these subterraneans take to live on, *viz.*, the aerial and ethereal parts—the most spiritous matter—for prolonging of life, such as *aquavitae* (if moderately taken) is among liquors, but leaving the terrestrial matter behind. The cure of such hurts is only for a human to seek out the "hole" with his finger, as if the spirits flowing from a man's warm hand were a sufficient antidote against their poisioned darts.

As birds and beasts—whose bodies are used to the changes in free and open air—foresee storms, so do those 'invisible people' have more sagacious (intellect) to understand by the "Books of Nature" about the things to come than we do; we are more pestered with the grosser dregs of all elementary mixtures and have our purer spirits choked by them.

The 'deer' scents out a man and (gun) powder (though a late invention) at a great distance; a hungry hunter, senses bread; and the raven, a carrion: their brains being long clarified by the high and subtle air and will detect a very small change. Thus, a man of 'Second Sight', perceiving the operations of these forecasting 'invisible people' among us (indulged through a stupendous providence to give warnings of some remarkable events, either in the air, earth, or waters), said he saw a winding-shroud creeping on a walking healthy person's legs until it came to the knee, and afterward it came up to the middle, then to shoulders, and at last over the head, which was not visible to anyone else. And by observing the spaces of time betwixt the several stages of is progression, he easily guessed how long the person was to live who wore the shroud—for when it finally approached the head, he said that such a person was ripe for the grave.

There are many places called '*Fairy-Hills*', which the 'mountain people' think impious and dangerous to peel or discover by taking earth or wood from them, superstitiously believing the "souls" of their predecessors dwell there. And for that end, they say, a mote or mount was dedicated beside every churchyard to receive the souls until their adjacent bodies arise, and so become as a '*Fairy-Hill*', since they use their bodies of air when called abroad. Their accounts affirm that creatures move invisibly in a house, and cast great stones, but do not cause hurt much because they are counterwrought by some more courteous and charitable spirits that are everywhere ready to defend humans (*Daniel 10.13*), to be souls that have not attained their rest through a vehement desire of revealing a murder or notable injury done or received, or a treasure that was forgot in their lifetime on earth, which when disclosed to the conjurer alone, the 'ghost' quite removes [itself].

In the next country to that of my former residence, around the year 1676, when there was some scarcity of grain, a marvelous vision struck the imagination of two women in one night, living at a good distance from one another, about a treasure hid in a hill called *sithbhruaich*, or *Fairy-Hill*. The appearance of a treasure was first represented to the fancy, and then an audible voice named the place where it was to their awoke senses. Whereupon both arose, and meeting accidentally at the place, learning of each others' purpose; and jointly digging, found a vessel as large as a Scottish pech, full of small pieces of good money, of ancient coin; which dividing betwixt them they sold in dish-fulls upon dish-fulls of meal to the country people.

But whether it was a 'good' or 'bad' angel, one of the subterranean people, or the restless soul of him who hid it that discovered it, and to what end it was done, I leave that to the examination of others.

These subterraneans have controversies, doubts, disputes, feuds, and party-sidings—there being some ignorance in all creatures and the vastest created intelligences not encompassing all things. As to vice and sin, whatever their own laws be, surely similar to ours, and equity, natural, civil, and revealed, they transgress and commit acts of injustice, and sin—by what is said prior as to their stealing of "nurses" to their children and other sorts of "kidnapping" or stealing our children away (who may heir to some estate in those invisible kingdoms), which never return. Surely, for the inconvenience of their *succubi*, who tryst with men, it is abominable. But, as for swearing and intemperance, they are not observed to be subject to those emotional irregularities of envy, spite, hypocrisy, lying and dissimulation.

Our religion obliges us not to make a preemptive and curious search into these abstrusenesses—so that the history of all ages gives as 'plain' of examples as possible of the extraordinary occurrences as make a modest inquiry not contemptible.

How much is written of pygmies, fairies, nymphs, sirens, apparitions, which though not the tenth part true, obviously could not spring from nothing?

Even English authors relate of '*Barry Island*', in Glamorganshire, that laying your ear into a cleft of the rocks, blowing of bellows, striking of hammers, clashing of armor, filing of irons will be heard distantly, ever since Merlin enchanted those subterranean *wights* to a solid manual forging of arms to *Aurelius Ambrosius* and his Britains until he returned—which Merlin being killed in a battle and not coming to loosen the knot, these active 'Vulcans' are there tied to a perpetual labor.

But to dip no deeper into this well, I will next give some account on how the 'seer', my informer, comes to have this secret way of correspondence beyond other mortals.

There are odd solemnities at investing a man with the privileges of the whole mystery of this 'Second Sight'. He must run a tether of hair (which bound a corpse to the bier) in a helix about his middle from end to end; then bow his head downwards, as did Elijah (1 *Kings* 18.42), and look back through his legs until he see a funeral advance till the people cross two marches, or look thus back through a hole where was a knot of 'fir'. But if the wind changes points while the hair tether is tied about him, he is in peril of his life.

The usual method for a curious person to get a transient sight of this otherwise invisible crew of subterraneans (if impotently or over-rashly sought) is to put his left foot under the wizard's right foot, and the seer's hand is put on the inquirers head, who is to look over the wizard's right shoulder (which has an ill appearance, as if, by this ceremony an implicit surrender were made of all betwixt the wizard's foot and his hand ere the person can be admitted *a privado* [an initiate] to the art).

Then will he see a multitude of *wights*, like furious hardy men flocking to him hastily from all quarters as thick as atoms in the air, which are no non-entities or phantasms (creatures proceeding from an frightened apprehension, confused or crazed sense), but realities, appearing to a stable human in his awakened senses and enduring a rational trial of their being. Those through fear strike him breathless and speechless.

The wizard, defending the lawfulness of his skill, forbids such horror, and comforts his novice by telling of *Zecharias*, being struck speechless at seeing apparitions (*Luke 1.20*).

Then he further maintains his art by vouching that *Elisha* to have had the same and disclosed it thus unto his servant (*2 Kings 6.17*) when blinded the Syrians, and *Peter* (in *Acts 5.9*) foreseeing the death of *Saphira* by perceiving it as a winding-sheet about her beforehand, and *Pail* (in *2 Corinthians 12.4*), who got a vision and sight as should not, nor could, be told. *Elisha* also in his chamber saw *Gehazi*, his servant, at a great distance, taking a reward from *Naaman* (in *2 Kings 5.26*).

Hence were the 'prophets' frequently called "seers"—or men of a "second" or more exalted sight than others. He acts for his purpose—also *Matthew 4.8*, where the devil undertakes to given even *Jesus* a sight of all nations and the finest things in the world at one glance, though in their natural situations and stations, were at a vast distance from another.

And it is said expressly that he did let him see them—and not in a map it seems, nor by a fantastical magical juggling of the sight, which he could not impose upon so discovering of a person. It would appear then to have been a sight of real solid substance and things of worth, which intended as a bait for his purposes.

Whence it might seem (comparing this relation of *Matthew 4.8* with the former) that the extraordinary or 'Second Sight' can be given by the ministry of bad as well as good spirits to those that will embrace it. And the instance of *Balaam* and the 'pythoness' [an oracle] makes it nothing less than probable.

Thus also the '*seer*' trains scholar by telling of the gradations of Nature, ordered by wise providence. And that men of the 'Second Sight' (being designed to give warnings against 'secret trappings') surpass the ordinary vision of other humans, which is a native (innate) habit in some, descended from their ancestors, and acquired as an 'artificial' improvement of their natural sight in others, resembling in their own kind a sort of artificial assistance like as with optic glasses—as prospectives, telescopes and microscopes.

Only with such supplementary aids, humans are treated here with an ability to perceive things that for their smallness or subtlety and secrecy are invisible to others, though they are in communication with the scientist daily. They have such a beam continually about them—as that of the sun—which when it shines clear only lets common eyes see the atoms in the air that without those rays they could not otherwise discern.

Some have the 'Second Sight' transmitted from [parents]—the whole family—without their consent or others teachings, proceeding only from a bounty of providence, it seems, or by some compact or a complex quality of the first acquirer.

The minor sort of *seers* prognosticate many future events, only for a month's space, from the shoulder-bone of a sheep on which a knife never came [and there is also something of this in the Ancient Near East] —for as before is said, *iron* hinders all the operations of those that travail in the intrigues of these hidden kingdoms. By looking into the bone, they will tell if whoredom be committed in the owner's house; what money the master of the sheep had; if any in that house will meet their death in that month; and if any cattle there will take ill. Then they will prescribe a preservative and prevention.

A woman singularly wise in these matters of foresight, living in *Colnasnach*, an isle of the *Hebrides* (in the time of the *Marquess of Montrose*, his wars with the states in Scotland), being notorious among many, and so examined by some that violently seized the isle, if she saw them coming or not, she said she saw them coming many hours before they came in view of the isle. But earnestly looking, she sometimes took them for enemies, sometimes for friends, and moreover they looked as if they went from the isle, not as men approaching it, which made her not put the inhabitants on their guard. The matter was that the barge wherein the enemy sailed was a little beforehand taken from the inhabitants of the same isle, and the men had their backs toward the isle when they were plying the oars towards it.

Thus this old scout and *Delphian Oracle* was at last deceived—and did deceive. Being asked who gave her such sights and such warnings, she said as soon as she set three "crosses" of straw upon the palm of her hand, a great ugly beast sprang up out of the earth near her and flew into the air. If what she inquired had success according to her wish, the beast would descend calmly and lick up the crosses. If it would not succeed, the beast would furiously thrust her and the crosses over on the ground and so vanish to his place.

Among other instances of undoubted verity proving in these the *beingness* of such aerial people or species of creatures not vulgarly known, I add the subsequent relations, some of which I have from my acquaintance with the actors and patients, and the rest from the eyewitnesses to the matter of fact.

The first whereof shall be of a woman taken out of her child-bed and having a lingering image of her substituted body in her room, which resemblance decayed, died and was buried—but the person stolen returning to her husband after two years' space, he being convinced by many undeniable tokens that she was his former wife, admitted her home and have diverse children by her.

Among other reports she gave her husband, this was one: that she perceived little what they did in the spacious house she lodged in until she anointed one of her eyes with a certain concoction that was by her; which they perceiving to have acquainted her with their actions, they fanned her blind in that eye with a puff of their breath. She found the place full of light, without any fountain or lamp from whence it did spring.

This person lived in the country next to that of my last residence and might furnish matter of dispute among *casuists* [*ethicists*], whether if her husband had been married in the interim of her two years' absence, he was obliged to divorce from the second spouse at the return of the first. There is an art, apparently without superstition, for recovering of such persons that are stolen, but think it superfluous to insert it.

I saw a woman of forty years of age and examined her (having another clergyman in my company) about a report that passed of her long fasting. It was told by them of the house, as well as herself, that she took very little or no food for several years past; that she tarried in the fields overnight, saw and conversed with a people she knew not, having wandered in seeking of her sheep and slept upon a hillock, and finding herself transported to another place before daybreak.

The woman had a child since that time and is still pretty melancholy and silent, hardly ever seen to laugh. Her natural heat and radical moisture seem to be equally balanced, like an unextinguished lamp, and going in a circle, not unlike the faint life of bees and some sort of birds that sleep all winter over and revive in the spring.

It is usual in all 'magical arts' to have the candidates prepossessed with the belief of their tutor's skill and ability to perform their feats and act their juggling pranks and 'slight of hand'—but a person called *Stewart* (possessed with a disbelief of the 'Second Sight' and living near my house), was so put it by a *seer* before many witnesses; he lost his speech, power of his legs and, breathing excessively as if expiring, because of many fearful *wights* that appeared to him, the company were forced to carry him home.

It is notorious spoken of about *Killin* within *Perthshire*, who fell tragically out with a yeoman [attendant of a noble household]—who coming into a company within an ale-house where a *seer* sat at the table, that at the sight of the entrant neighbor, the *seer*, startlingly rose to go out of the house; and being asked the reason of his haste, told that the entrant man would die within two days—at which news the named entrant stabbed the *seer* and was himself executed two days after for the fact.

A minister, very intelligent but misbelieving all such sights as were not ordinary, chancing to be in a narrow lane with a *seer*, who perceived a *wight* of a known visage furiously to encounter them, the *seer* desired the minister to turn out of the way, who scorning his reason and holding himself in the path with them when the *seer* was going hastily out of the way—they were both violently case aside to a good distance, and the fall made them lame for the rest of their life. A little after the minister was carried home, the 'death-toll' rang for the man whose representation had met them in the narrow path some half an hour before.

Another example is a *seer* in *Kintyre* in Scotland, sitting at a table with diverse others,
suddenly did cast his head aside. The company asking him why he did it, he answered
that such a friend of his, by name, then in
Ireland, threatened immediately to cast a
dish-full of butter in his face. The men
wrote down the day and hour and sent to
the gentleman to know the truth, which
deed the gentleman declared he did at that
very time, for he knew that his friend was a
seer and would make sport with it. The men
that were present and examined the matter
exactly, told me this story and withal that a
seer would, with all his optics, perceive no
other object so readily as this at such a distance.

[*Kirk's primary manuscript ends here.*]

of the predictions made by seers[*]

My Lord, after narrow inquisition, have discovered many true and remarkable observations on the subject of the 'Second Sight'.

Firstly, that this sight is not criminal, since a man can come by it unawares and without his consent. But it is certain that he will see more fatal and fearful things than he will gladsome.

Secondly, the *seers* avouch that several who go to the *siths* (or people at rest, and, in respect to us, in peace) before the natural period of their lives expire, do frequently appear to them.

Thirdly, a vehement desire to attain this art is very helpful to the inquirer, and the species of an absent friend, which appears to the *seers* as clearly as if he had sent his lively picture to present itself before him, is

---

[*] This discourse is attached to Kirk's manuscript, in regards to "a succinct account of My Lord Tarbett's relations in a letter to the Honorable Robert Boyle, Esquire" as given in the original edition.

no fantastic shadow of a sick apprehension, but a reality and a messenger coming for unknown reasons; not from the original similitude of itself, but from a more swift and pragmatic people that recreate themselves in offering secret intelligence to men, though generally they are unacquainted with that kind of correspondence, as if they had lived in a different element from them.

Fourthly, I presume to day that this sight can be no quality of air nor of the eyes, because: such as live in the same air and see all other things as far off and as clearly, yet have not the 'Second Sight'; a *seer* can give another person this sight transiently by putting his hand and foot in the posture he resuires of him; the unsullied eyes of infants can naturally perceive no new unaccustomed objects but what appear to other men, unless exalted and clarified in some way, as Balaam's donkey* for a time (though

---

* In *Numbers 22:21-39*, Balaam's donkey diverts from the trail, blocked by the 'Angel of the Lord' and Balaam beats the donkey, to which God says "if your donkey had not seen me and diverted, I would have killed you and spared the donkey."

in a witch's eye, the beholder cannot see his own image reflected, as is visible in the eyes of other people).

Fifthly, since the things seen by *seers* are real entities, the passages and predictions found true, but a few endowed with this sight and whose not of bad lives or addicted to malefices, the true solution of the phenomenon seems rather to be the courteous endeavors of our fellow creatures in the invisible world to convince us (in opposition to *Sadduce's*, *Socinians*, and atheists) of a deity, of spirits, of a possible and harmless method of correspondence betwixt men and them even in this life, of their operations for our caution and warning, of the orders and degrees of angels, whereof one order with bodies of air condensed and curiously shaped may be next to a human, superior to them in understanding yet unconfirmed, and of their region, habitation and influence on man, greater than that of stars on inanimate bodies; a knowledge (belike) reserved for these last atheistic ages, wherein the profanity of human lives has debauched and blinded their understanding as to the prophets and regions of the dead.

Nor does the ceasing of the visions upon the *seer's* transmigration into foreign kingdoms confirms greatly my account of an invisible people, guardian over and careful of men, who have their different offices and abilities in distinct countries (as in *Daniel 10.13*), Israel's, Grecia's, and Persia's assistant princes, whereof who so prevails, give the dominion and ascendant to his pupils and vassals over the opposite armies and kingdom having their topical spirits or powers assisting and governing them, the Scottish *seer* banished to the Americas, being a stranger there as well to the invisible as to the visible inhabitants and wanting a familiarity of his former correspondents, he could not have the favor and warnings, by the several visions and predictions which were wont to be granted him by these acquaintances and favorites in his own country.

For if what he wanted to see were realities (as I have made appear), it would be too great an honor for Scotland to have such seldom-seen watchers and predominant powers over it alone, acting in it so expressly, and all other nations wholly destitute of the like; though without all peradventure, all other people wanted the right *key* of their *cabinet* and the exact method for corresponding with them, except the sagacious active Scots, as many of whom have retained it for a long, and by surprises and raptures do often foretell what in kindness is really represented to them at several occasions. To which purpose, the learned lynx-eyed Mr. Baxter (on *Revelation 12.7*), writing of the fight between Michael and the Dragon, gives a very pertinent note, *viz.* that he knows not but ere any great action (especially tragical) is done on earth, that first the battle and victory is acted and achieved in the air between the good and evil spirits.

It seems these were the human's guardians, and similar battles are oftentimes perceived aloft in the night time, the event of which might easily be represented by someone of the number correspondent on earth, as frequently the report of great actions have been more swiftly carried to other countries than all of the art of us mortals could possibly dispatch it.

Saint Augustine (on *Mark 9.4*) gives no small intonation of this truth, averring that *Elias* appeared with *Jesus* on the Mount in his proper body; but *Moses* in an aerial body, assumed like the angels who appeared, and had the ability to eat with *Abraham*, though no necessity on the account of their bodies, as likewise the late doctrine of the preexistence of "souls" living into aerial vehicles, gives a singular hint of the possibility of the thing, if not direct proof of the whole assertion; which moreover may be illuminated by diverse other instances of the like nature and as wonderful, besides what I said above.

Sixthly, the invisible *wights* which haunt houses seem rather to be some of our subterranean inhabitants (which appear often to those with the 'Second Sight'), rather than 'evil spirits' or 'devils', because they throw great stones, pieces of earth and wood at the inhabitants without hurting them, as if they acted not maliciously like 'devils' but in sport like buffoons.

All ages have afforded some obscure testimonies of it: as Pythagoras, his doctrine of transmigration; Socrates's *Daemon* that gave him warning of future dangers; Plato's classifying them into various vehiculated species of spirits; Dionysius Areopagitica's marshaling nine orders of spirits, superior and subordinate; the poets, their borrowing of the philosophers and adding their own fancies of fountain, river, and sea nymphs, wood, hill, and mountain inhabitants, and that every place and thing in cities and countries has special invisible regular gods and governors.

Cardano speaks of his father, his seeing the species of his friend in a moonshine night riding fiercely by his window on a white horse the very night his friend died at a vast distance from him, by which he understood that some alteration would suddenly ensue. Cornelius Agrippa and the learned Dr. More have several passages tending that way.

The noctambulos* themselves would appear to have some foreign joking spirit possessing and supporting them when they walk

---

* Latin for 'night-walker'; a 'night owl' or someone that stays up late (into the nighttime hours). The reference here seems to be of "*sleep-walking.*"

on deep waters and tops of houses without danger when asleep in the dark. For it was no way probable that mere apprehension and strong imagination, setting the animal spirits at work to move the body, could preserve it from sinking in the deep or falling down headlong when asleep anymore than when awake, the body being then as ponderous as before; and it is hard to attribute it to a spirit flatly evil and enemy to man, because the *noctambulo* returns to his own place safe.

And the most furious tribe of the *daemons* are not permitted by providence to attack men so frequently either by night or by day: for in the Highlands, as there may be many fair ladies of this aerial order which do often tryst with lascivious young men in the quality of *succubi* or lightsome paramours and strumpets (called *leannain sith*, or familiar spirits in *Deuteronomy 18.11*), so do many of our Highlanders, as if astrangling by nightmare, pressed with a fearful dream, or rather possessed by one of our aerial neighbors rise up fierce in the night and apprehending the nearest weapons, do push and thrust at all person in the same room with them, sometimes even wounding their own comrades to death, the like whereof fell sadly out within a few miles of me at the writing hereof.

I add but one instance more of a very young maid who lived near to my last residence, that in one night learned a large piece of poesy by the frequent repetition of it from one of our nimble and courteous spirits, whereof a part was pious, the rest superstitious (for I have a copy of it), and no other person was ever heard to repeat it before, nor was the mail capable to compose it of herself.

Finally, having demonstrated and made evident to sense this extraordinary vision of our tramontane *seers* and what is seen by them by what is said above, many having seen this same *spectres* and apparitions at once, having their visive faculties entire; for *non est disputandum de gustu*, it now remains to show that it is not unsuitable to reason not the Holy Scriptures.

First, that it is not repugnant to reason: doth appear from this that it is no less strange for immortal sparks and souls to come and be immersed into gross terrestrial elemental bodies and be so propagated, so nourished, so fed, so clothed as they are, and breathe in such an air and world prepared for them, than for Hollanders, or hollow-cavern inhabitants, to live and traffic among us in another state of being without our knowledge.

For Raymond de Subinde, in his third book, chapter 12, argues quaintly that all sorts of living creatures have a happy rational polity of their own with great contentment, which government and mutual converse of theirs they all pride and plume themselves because it is as unknown to man, as man is to them. Much more, that the Son of the Highest Spirit should assume a body like ours convinces all the world that no other thing that is possible needs be much wondered at.

The *manucodiata*, or 'bird of paradise', living in the highest region of the air; common birds in the second region; flies and insects in the lowest; humans and beasts on the earth's surface; worms, otters, badgers, in waters; likewise, Hell is inhabited at the centre and Heaven in the circumference; can we then think the middle cavities of the earth empty?

Further, let us take up all that remains to us now—to answer the obvious objections against the reality and lawfulness of my speculations.

QUESTION 1: How do you salve the 'Second Sight' from compacts and witchcraft?

ANSWER: Though this correspondence with the intermediate unconfirmed people (betwixt man and angel) be not ordinary to all of us who are 'superterraineans', yet this sight falling to some persons by accident and its being connatural to others from their birth, the derivation of it cannot always be wicked. A too great curiosity indeed to acquire any unnecessary art may be blameworthy, but diverse of the secret commonwealth may be permission discover themselves as innocently to us, who are in another state, as some of us men do to fishes, which are in another element, when we plunge and dive into the bottom of the seas, their native region; and in process of time we may come to converse as familiarity with those nimble and agile clans (but with greater pleasure and profit) as we do now with the Chinese and Antipodes.

QUESTION 2: Are they subject to vice, lusts, passion, and injustice as we who live on the surface of the earth?

ANSWER: The *seer* tells us that these wandering aerial people have no such an impetus and fatal tendency to any vice as men, as not being drenched into so gross and dreggy bodies as we, but yet are in an imperfect state, and some of them making better essays for heroic actions than others, having the same measures of virtue and vice as we, and still expecting advancement to a higher more splendid state of life.

One of them is stronger than many humans, yet are not inclined to hurt mankind, except by commission for a gross misdemeanor, as the destroying angel of Egypt and the Assyrians (*Exodus 12.29, 2 Kings 19.35*). They haunt most where is most barbarity, and therefore our ignorant ancestor to prevent the insults of that strange people used as rude and coarse a remedy; such as exorcisms, donations and vows.

But how soon ever the true piety prevailed in any place, it did not put the inhabitants beyond the reach and authority of those subtle inferior co-inhabitants and colleagues of ours: the Father of all Spirits and the person himself having the only command of his soul and actions. A concurrence they may have to what is virtuously done, for upon committing of a foul deed, one will find a demur upon his soul, as if his cheerful colleague had deserted him.

QUESTION 3: Do these airy tribes procreate? If so, how are they nourished and at what period of time do they die?

ANSWER: Supposing all spirits to be created at once in the beginning, souls to preexist and to circle about into several states of probationship to make them either totally inexcusable or perfectly happy against the last day, solves at the difficulties.

But in every deed, and speaking suitable to the nature of things, there is no more absurdity for a spirit to inform an infantine in body of air than a body composed of dull and drowsy earth, the best of spirits have always delighted more to appear into aerial than into terrestrial bodies. They feed mostly on quintessences and ethereal essences.

Now the air being a body as well as earth, no reason can be given why there may not be particles of more vivific spirit formed of it for procreation than is possible to be of earth, which takes more time and pains to rarify and ripen it ere it can come to have a prolific virtue. And if our aping darlings did not thus procreate, their whole number would be exhausted after a considerable space of time.

For they are of more refined bodies and intellectuals than we, and of far less heavy and corruptive humours (which cause a dissolution), yet many of their lives being dissonant to right reason and their own laws and their vehicles not being wholly free of lust and passion, especially of the most spiritual and haughty sins, they pass (after a long healthy life) into an orb and receptacle fitted for their degree until they come under the general cognizance of the last day.

APPENDIX

Materials reprinted from
"*The Secret Book of Elven-Faerie*"
for convenient reference.

APPENDIX

the secret world of elven-faerie {abridged}

Following the rise of the Sons of Mil—the rise of human populations in Keltia—most mystically inclined members of Elven and Faerie races "transitioned" into the Otherworld, though the legacy of Druidism continued on in public forms until the time of Saint Patrick and the "Elven Holocaust" or Dark Ages. After focused persecution lifted and many diabolical laws were repealed, the possession of "wizarding blood"—and the practice of magic—no longer carried a death sentence. Yet, by this new era of "enlightenment," dilution of Elven lore and Faerie ancestry dissolved contemporary human understanding of the subject, reducing it to the best that remains from the Grimm family collection as "fable" and "fantasy."

The Elven Way and Faerie Faith were not altogether lost. As a world revival of druidry or "neodruidism" emerged, more remnants of the ancient way started receiving attention, and even documentation. The original of these pertain mainly to daily magical rural living—the traditions that earth-oriented and Nature-based druids and "neopagans" frequently follow today.

In contemporary lore, and even in some New Age interpretations, the term "Elven" is applied a catch-all category for a host of ancestral spirits, Nature-spirits and elemental spirits aligned to a combination of earth and air forces. Some types occur in cultural traditions including *Dark Elves* of the *Unseelie Court*, misunderstood "devas," the *"Sidhe"* or *High Elves* of the *Seelie Court*, the *Linchetto* of Etruscan-Italy, the *Quendi* of Sumerian *Eridu* and finally, *Silvani/Sylph* woodland inhabiting Nature guardians— sometimes called *Wood Elves*.

Modern ritual and "practical magick" systems are aligned to "elemental magick" and elemental currents of energy that share affinity with specific "elementals"—the spiritual forms taken by "transitioned" Elves and Faerie Folk. These entities—appropriated to the "astral plane"—are called in ceremonial and ritual magick at the appropriate corners of the nemeton or ritual circle. In the Edaphic tradition influencing this current book, "Elves" usually replace the traditional gnomes as "guardians of the north." In a similar fashion, "Dragons" or "Fire-Drakes" may replace the djinn. There are other types of elemental entities that may be incorporated with ritual magic and/or daily magical living, as described within this chapter.

Lore of "Changelings" appear frequently in connection to traditional Elven-Ffayrie history—and although we do not know its definitive source, it is carried in worldwide belief systems.

"Changelings" are fundamentally human replacements, often newborns, which are switched with an "elf-child." That the Faerie races share a "low reproductive rate" is one driving theory behind this lore—therefore maintaining their populations and/or evolving their genetic diversity by occasionally "stealing humans." It is also possible that this lore applies to phenomenon attributed to many "Otherworldly beings" even in alternative culture today, although we choose contemporary semantics reflecting our technological knowledge, such as:"alien babies," "cloning" and "DNA harvesting." However, throughout the Dark Ages of the Church, religious beliefs maintained that sickly children and infant deaths were all consequences of faerie—or demonic—assault.

"Changeling Theory" is not restricted only to newborns and children—although the archetype of the "stolen child" is the most iconic. Direct interactions between Elven-Ffayrie and Humans are not common—sexual unions between them even less so.

The only instance of "fairy theft" in the current Edaphic tradition is the lore of "*transignation*"—when someone may not be willing or even aware of themselves being used as a simulacrum host for a "walk-in" entity.

In anthropological examinations of Elven-Ffayrie by *W.Y. Wentz,* another theory regarding "fairy theft" is put forth. It is possible—as he suggests—that after Milesian

---

* W.Y. Wentz *"Fairy-Faith in Celtic Countries."*

humans invade and attempt to entrap the Danubian race (before their flight for hills and caves), that the Fae occasionally kidnapped unattended off-spring of the people who had conquered them. It is also theoretically possible that the later historical Elvish Drwyds themselves, after being driven underground to hide in the dense forests and old groves, may have kidnapped potential apprentices to raise and pass down their knowledge and wisdom to, before returning them to Human society.

When we examine other more recent historical cases like that of *Rev. Robert Kirk*—and perhaps *Thomas Rhymer* and others—we know that select mortals (perhaps even of Elven-Ffayrie lineage) have been taken to the "Otherworld Faerieland." Our primary examples of Faerie-lore, when Otherworld beings interact with mortals, all take place in a surreal yet vividly tangible manner. We know that the Elementals are capable of imbuing all types of life with their spirit. There is also lore regarding their ability to use simulacra from birth or "walk-in" at some point during the person's "more able" years, such as puberty. Either of these abiliities—'transition' or 'transignation'—would require, what we would consider (at this level or gradient of understanding and vocabulary), incredibly powerful and advanced "magical abilities" to perform; especially to result in permanent effects.

Elves and Ffayrie have abilities to disorient wanderers that happen upon enchanted fey woods. This belief inspired an old saying: *"Faerie folk live in old oaks."* Surviving superstition inspires warned travelers passing through such forests to wear their cloaks backwards, or inside out (reversed) to ward against enchantments and glamours that might get a person lost. It is even possible that doing such would "subconsciously" increase one's present "awareness."

Clouds, heavy mist and dense fog are all natural threshold conditions related to the Otherworld and Elven-Ffayrie. Just as many unsuspecting travelers might get lost, there is a long-standing magical tradition of using fog to aid physical access the Otherworld. Lore suggests that these 'twilight' misty conditions create a conduit of communication between worlds that may be employed from either side. And while misleading wanderers through a forest might at first seem malicious, it is possible that Elven-Ffayrie beings make efforts to keep people away from certain locales, powerful thresholds or even dimensional portals and "star-gates" between worlds.

According to the accounts of *Rev. Robert Kirk*, the Sidhe Court resided in a particular faerie "mound," "hill" or *"howe"* at that time. When describing the space/time of the Otherworld Faerieland, Kirk found that, in his experience of it, the Otherworld was far too vast to have been contained within a single hill—providing early examples of "hyperspace" or a "fourth spatial dimension." Interestingly, many of these "Hollowed Hills" were ancient burial sites of Elven-Ffayrie ancestors once residing on the surface world.

The *"Tuatha D'Anu"* and other royal-fey bloodlines would preserve the remains of their ancestors in "tomb-hills." And although not used for burial, funerary rites of the "Ancient Mystery School" were practiced in "pyramids" and "ziggurats"—artificial "hills" or mountains with cave-like chambers built in places that did not have these naturally occurring landforms. This motif also lends some "Gothic" overtones, inspiring other related mystical traditions emphasizing the more "vampyric" themes and semantics.

Elven Tradition is revived in Druidism, but it is not the same as the magic practiced by Humans—which employs these other beings to lend their Otherworldly powers to Human ritual. It is from Human lore *about* Elves—based on Human perception and vocabulary of "other" worlds—that we find terms like "Middle Earth," "Mid-branch," and "Middle-world"—all of which imply the third-dimensional plane.

Each "point" in Middle Earth (physical space) has a center, called "*midhe.*" This center is connected to an ethereal "Recursive Spiral" of cosmic energy where space/time ascends and descends, coiling into upper and lower frequencies/dimensions, ultimately unifying all things—but at different perceptual or semantic levels of understanding or classification. But they are connected *All-as-One*.

Make no mistakes here in thinking of the spiral-like Multiverse in absolute terms of "upper" and "lower" worlds. We use this terminology as only an abstract differentiation to describe the effect or relationship we perceive as one plane or level of existence with another—but they are all connected together. If we apply modern scientific vocabulary and hyper-geometry in our view of an "Infinite" Universe or Multiverse, than we must accept that there are infinite "smaller/lower" or "larger/upper" levels of existence or dimensions. Elven lore even suggests a type of hyperspace existence that is subjective to experience—particularly as Humans define "time."

The "Lands Below"—as Robert Kirk experienced them—possessed its own moon, stars, and even a sun similar to Earth's. He explained that by appearance, everything seemed more vividly real than even the physical world. *So... the "Hollow Hills" have their own sky..?* Remember that the Otherworld—that which is unseen from our view of reality or has not collapsed or condensed into our reality—is indeed without limit.

When we confine our semantics to the mortal view of reality, the limitlessness of existence is collapsed in "our" dimension as various natural conditions that we can observe within our range of "awareness." Some of these are considered "portals" or "thresholds" because they allow for a more fluid exchange of energies between worlds —or else, between degrees of 'perception' and 'reality' for the same singular "world."

Specific conditions promote specific types of inter-dimensional energetic activity, which affects both the "external" world we are experiencing and the "internal" mental set doing the experiencing—a further example that these "two" facets are really one and the same spectrum of energy: that our "internal" and "external" worlds are One.

Cross-quarter 'thresholds'—the 'equinoxes' and 'solstices'—share qualities from other "degrees" of reality-experience (semantics), such as 'astronomical' alignment, or 'electromagnetic fields' around earth, but they are most often distinguished in Druidic tradition as the "Four Albans"—or *Four Lights*—

which compose at least half of the Celtic "Grove Festivals" revived in modern "neo-paganism" today. Springtime—between the Spring Equinox and Summer Solstice—is traditionally the most active period of the year for elemental Nature-spirits. Beltane (May's Eve) and Midsummer's Eve are particularly famous times for "Faerie Rade." Note that *Beltane* (May's Eve) and *Samhain* (ancient "Halloween") also mark periods of peak inter-dimensional activity—times that correspond to the setting and rise of the Pleiades (respectively).

Another facet of inter-dimensional "fairy lore" is called the "fairy ring"—naturally occurring circles or rings found on the ground in Nature that are set apart from its natural surrounding. Often this manifests as a bit of grass that grows higher or darker, forming a ring—usually only a few feet in diameter—or it may be a ring of mushrooms. Traditionally, these "Faerie-Rings" are signs of not only Elven-Ffayrie activity in an area, but also places in which a transition into—or from—the "Otherworld" is likely or has already occurred.

The physical appearance—and physical explanations—of "Faerie-Rings" (and other natural or observable phenomenon) does not eliminate the existence of energetic activity that may be "perturbing" what we can see, but from beneath the surface of our awareness and understanding. It is also curious to note that Humans have experienced "alien" and "fairy" encounters under psychoactive effects of mushrooms, DMT and other hallucinogenic substances. It is possible that some of the receptors activated in the brain as a result of their use do allow for a "wider range" of perceptual experience of reality—but there are no guarantees that these "external" methods will result in Self-Honest experiences. Wizards suggest that falling asleep in a Faerie-Ring or on an Elven-Mound will increase your chances of Otherworld contact—possibly due to a presence of spores, *who knows?* Other folklore suggests that if you run around one nine times you will do the same—*kicking up more spores?*

One of the main issues—for Humans—regarding physically transitioning into the Otherworld, relates to inept faculties to not only sense "portal frequencies," but also adjust personal vibrations to successfully "transition" into other existential states. Most Humans do not carry an awareness of the energetic matrix we occupy, then alone possess an understanding of its influence— such is, and always has been, the main focus of the "wizarding ways" and high mystical arts. In other instances and occult practices, similar results may be obtained using "astral projection" and other experimental practices—frequency shifts in consciousness where the physical body is not transported, yet we can mentally experience it because everything is connected— our consciousness is already connected to the ALL. Our sensory faculties are simply limited to a specific range of an infinite spectrum of energies.

The cosmic spectrum of infinite potentiality includes many possible frequencies in existence "above" and "below" what Humans are normally capable of sensing. While these various degrees might be perceived and classified as separate "levels" in exclusion to one another, the separation exists only in consciousness—there is no actual separation between a subject and the individual doing the observing; there is only one singular reality.

Each "degree" of vision—each magnification of the microscope—yields only one "degree" of awareness, data and knowledge, but it is not the only "degree" of possible understanding, nor is it likely to be the true holistic totality of a "thing"—since we are always going to classify "things" in exclusion to all other "things."

Another energetic interaction taking place between worlds is called an "Elf-Shot." If someone—typically a Human—is hit by an arrowhead from an Elf or Faerie being, we call them "Elf-Shot." This lore is the subject of some controversy in the New Age and as a result is not frequently discussed. The tradition holds, however, that one of the consequences of being struck by such an arrow is some degree of "Faerie-Sight"—or, at the very least, the ability to see the fey that shot you.

Rarer, but more serious, consequences of "Elf-Shot" include permanent "transitions" to the Otherworld or "Faerieland"—which other Humans, in many instances, would only see as 'death', because the "body" often remains in the physical world. This may not even occur overnight and might first be recognized as an illness that purges impurities of the physical body so that its spirit can be free. Keep in mind: this is not something that may be self-induced. In fact, it usually only happens unintentionally—because Elven Courts seldom assist Humans in "seeing them" or "inviting" them to their world.

Sometimes an "Elf-Shot" occurs when a Human just happens to be in the line of fire between rivaling courts—such as the *Seelie* and *Unseelie*. It is also possible that an "Elf-Shot" victim is struck without knowing it has occurred—so if they are not perceptive, they may not see the fey that shot them. Even if it does not produce an illness, it has been known to inadvertently have other unpleasant side-effects—such as promoting discord between friends and neighbors.

"Foison" is a common game where members of the fey will "steal" Human food. This should not to be misinterpreted as an act of malevolence—it *is* a "game." Lore suggests that they only eat the essence of Human food and not the foods themselves—possibly lending to the "thin" "angelic" "ethereal" descriptions carried by many of the types. As a result, they will absorb only what is necessary from foodstuff—leaving the remains often without nutrients. There are reports from farmers in Celtic Countries where the insides of their stalks are carefully eaten while leaving outsides intact and whole. Modern folk might just think it is a result of some pests, but often it does not seem eaten, rotted, infested or touched.

According to lore, foods prepared in Faerieland are the most exquisite—pure natural and organic essences drawn from the sweetest life-giving nectar of the Green World. One popular belief is that if you eat any foods during your stay in the Otherworld, you may find yourself trapped there. Although *Rev. Robert Kirk* was eventually trapped in Faerieland, it was not a result of eating the food there. He had tasted it and still continued to "transition" back and forth between worlds several times. However, he reports to us that the "want" or "memory" of it lingered perpetually and could not be equaled in the physical world.

Cuneiform Tablets describe an exchange between Enki and Adapa—where Enki instructs Adapa on the dangers of eating the "Food of Death" when visiting the "Otherworld," though Anu eventually offers Adapa the "Food of Life" and it is refused because of Enki's instructions. Had he eaten of it, the Human race would have been "as like the gods."

The "Geirt Coimitheth" or "Just-Halver" is an anomaly of the Otherworld. Its titles are references to its abilities and function—called a "joint-eater" or "marrow-eater"—a reference to it feeding on energy or essences of humans; possibly even a human Elven-Ffayrie Simulacra. Humans will "live-to-eat" or eat for pleasure, while the fey generally just eat-to-live and take only what essences and nutrients are necessary for survival. A "Geirt Coimitheth" is really a shadow—or the shadow of a person—a "co-walker" that feeds on what the host eats.

With a lack of substance in ethereal/astral planes, there is a shortage of food-stuff—

but memory of such remains. Those who maintain food and drug addictions in the physical world find great difficulty satisfying these cravings in a spiritual dimension. Addictions conditioned on the mind and spirit can actually remain in tact after one's physical lifetime, but are not ever satisfied. While truly ethereal beings have no need to eat physical substances, Elven-Faerie beings are not indigenous to the Astral World and once ate regularly as we do.

"Co-walkers" are Elven-Ffayrie creatures that walk invisibly in the Middle World of humans in disguise. They take on human form—'Simulacrum Transignation'—or they can simply take the appearance of a human. Like all elementals, they reserve a right to remain invisible—yet present—or to mimic surrounding and camouflage themselves. These abilities may also be used to assume animal forms.

The "Giert Coimitheth" is just one example of a co-walker that shadows a human form. Others exist as well—some not so clearly classified—that simply shadow Elvish descendents or assume a full "transignation" or "walk-in" using physical simulacra. There is still a lot of debate about the semantics and vocabulary that should be used for this spiritual phenomenon. Other lore suggests that the co-walker may act as a "spirit-guide," guardian *"ang-elf"* or "co-magician." They may also be of any elemental type.

Elves of the Unseelie Court share many attributes with their relatives of the Light. Their appearance is tall and slender like the Sylvan Elves, with their long angular and hardened faces set in humorless stoic expressions. Their eyes appear small, squinted, and hollow—yet burning and piercing. They are used to residing in a Realm of Darkness and make habitats in larger underground subterranean labyrinths and caves. "Dark Elves" typically lead solitary lives, but there is large capital city for the Unseelie Court, as reported by *Rev. Robert Kirk* in his journals and secret writings.

"Dark Elves" are so-called because they are no longer one-to-one with the "Tribe of Starlight." They are set apart—exiled from the Seelie Court—taking their lives to even further "underground crevices." They are still "fey-folk," but submission to anger and brooding has left many of them blinded to pursuits of harmony and ascension.

There are modern references to Dark Elves, calling them *"Drow"*—rhymes with "cow"—yet this word does not appear in ancient Elvish languages. But, there is, however, the ancient word *"Daetenin"*—meaning "Dark-Dragon folk"—and the Unseelie word *"Ishmaen,"* which is an Elven slur towards Wizards and Druids that have perverted their magical birthright.

"Dark Elves" are not inherently evil—they simply seem to remain perpetually embittered about their conditions of existence as a result of the "Rise of Humans." It is this very subject that drew a dividing line between Seelie and Unseelie Courts—which were originally the same race before the Rise of Humans and the Underground "transition."

Would

you

like

to

know

more

???

*Discover other volumes in the Elvenomicon
Druid's Pocket Forest Library.*

*Such as
"The Enchanted Forest" and
"Book of Ogham"*

CLASSICS OF MARDUKITE MESOPOTAMIA
REVISED HARDCOVER 2-VOLUME SET

SUMERIAN RELIGION

Introducing the Anunnaki Gods
of Mesopotamian Neopaganism

Mardukite Liber-50

by Joshua Free

BABYLONIAN MYTH & MAGIC

Spiritual Traditions and Mysticism
in Mesopotamian Anunnaki Religion

Mardukite Liber-51+E

by Joshua Free

SYSTEMOLOGY BASICS HARDCOVER SET

THE POWER OF ZU

Applying Mardukite Zuism and
Systemology to Everyday Life
Systemology Liber-S1-Z
based on a classic lecture series
by Joshua Free

THE WAY INTO THE FUTURE

A Handbook for the New Human
Systemology Liber-S1-W
collected works mini-anthology
by Joshua Free

CRYSTAL CLEAR

(Handbook for Seekers)

Mardukite Systemology Liber-2B
by Joshua Free

Take control of your destiny
and chart the first steps
toward your own spiritual evolution.
Realize new potentials of the
Human Condition with
a Self-guiding handbook for
Self-Processing toward
Self-Actualization
in Self-Honesty using actual
techniques and training
provided for the coveted
"Mardukite Systemology Grade-III
Self-Defragmentation Course Program"
—once only available
directly and privately from
the underground Systemology Society.

Discover the amazing power behind the
applied spiritual technology
used for counseling and advisement in
the tradition of Mardukite Zuism.

19 95   20 20

JOSHUA FREE

PUBLISHED BY THE **JOSHUA FREE** IMPRINT REPRESENTING

The Mardukite Academy of Systemology

THE JOSHUA FREE IMPRINT
JFI PUBLICATIONS

MARDUKITE
ZUISM

mardukite.com

www.ingramcontent.com/pod-product-compliance
Lightning Source LLC
Chambersburg PA
CBHW011223120626
46545CB00010B/3122